HOW TO START A FREELANCE BUSINESS IN AUSTRALIA

Jennifer Lancaster

First edition 2010. Second edition 2017.
Published by Power of Words, Australia.

A catalogue record for this book is available from the National Library of Australia. Subject: Starting a Business.

Give feedback on the book: sales@powerofwords.com.au, or on Goodreads. See **www.jenniferlancaster.com.au/books** for ebook version.

ISBN 13: 978-0-9945105-1-8

Contents

About the Author: Jennifer Lancaster

After many years freelancing in copywriting and editing, I finally learned that planning a niche, promoting yourself, and continuing action does result in success!

Sure, it's a challenging way to make a living. I found challenges within and the wrong roads to take. The reason I persist is so that I can 'make a living but have a life' and be available for my family. Both my husband and I work from home in Queensland.

Since 2010, the world of freelancing and getting work has changed. So much of it is about your online presence and creating connections both online and offline. Three years ago I put even more tips learned whilst marketing into my book: ***Power Marketing: An Aussie Guide to Business Growth***.

I hope you enjoy my many hours of research.

Introduction

Congratulations on taking your first steps into the great unknown of being your own boss. Usually you can set up a freelance or consulting business from home. In many ways, working at home is a great advantage, and at times it is a disadvantage.

As you move from an employee mindset to a self-employed mindset, you might discover that <u>energy</u> and <u>self-discipline</u> is key. Among the challenges of new freelancers is <u>finding enough clients</u>.

Within these pages you will get an idea of the different areas of freelancing, how to find your niche, how a provider markets their services, and how to manage income and costs.

Just as I found when starting out, you will find the major challenges are from within. It is hard to keep <u>motivated</u> and <u>focussed</u> when working alone. That's why I have included some helpful tips to manage your time, set meaningful goals, and plan your finances in the first very tough months.

As you build up your "trust" account with businesspeople, you will find that your savings account, and *your confidence*, grows with it. Remember, your service's worth relates to the value you add to others' lives and businesses. So let's step up your intrinsic value!

Why Do YOU Want to Run a Freelance Business?

10 Reasons a Service Business is Better than a JOB

1. *The security you perceive in a job is not really there*. Needing security, those made redundant dismiss any ideas they had of starting their own service business. They think "I'll just do this menial job for a while to get by". Unfortunately, these days there is no such thing as a secure job, so you might as well be doing something you love.

2. *I need income right now*. The newly redundant worker will take quite some time to land a job. Instead of being downbeat, you can create some freelance income within three to four weeks.

3. *Outsourcers don't have to be young*. Some employers are 'ageist' and if you are in the 40-70 range, you might really come up against it. But harried small business owners or marketing managers are not that interested in your age, gender, or whether you're a mother with a crazy schedule… but they do want their problems solved. Usually, they are open to outsourcing different aspects of business that are too hard and too time-consuming for their staff to do.

4. *You will have a better quality of life by freelancing*. There is flexibility in that you can choose to work fewer hours than normal, at the times you need. You can run a service business only working 12 hours per week and some nights, if you really

wish to. Or you can work (with meetings as well) 40 hours per week and earn a really good income, depending on your level of skill.

5. *Become an expert and bring in the cash cows.* Everyone knows that specialised information is highly sought. Experience helps, but so does a lot of learning and writing up your own programs, books, or courses.*

6. *Service businesses do not need high overheads or capital.* Unlike a bricks & mortar business, you will operate out of home and so your main costs include: mobile phone, internet, business cards, software, the odd development course, and networking functions. Plus, if meeting people, a few dollars for petrol.

7. *No boss to answer to.* Your clients will be the ones you have to please, but they come and go. You can take a week off if you want to.

8. *No wasted time commuting.* Also save time on office gossip, longwinded meetings, and incidental emails. All going to plan, you can be a lot more productive. 'Spare time' can be spent in the betterment of your skills.

9. *Be there for your family.* For many people, this is the most important factor. If your little one is sick, you won't feel guilty for staying home, and in school holidays you can reduce the workload a bit to spend time with the kids. (Perhaps working at night to maintain your clients).

10. *You can finally pursue the dream career you have been putting off.* If your spouse is working or you have gotten a large payout,

you have some breathing space to learn and grow in a new line of work.

* While you are beginning your freelancing service and it is still quiet, it's beneficial to create an information product or sell online advertising that will bring in a steady cash flow. It also aids your credibility – if you choose the right type of products.

Your planned passive income will be very handy when the client work is slow, so plan some time out of your week to do this too.

7 Reasons Why Starting a Service Business May Not Be for You

1. If you dislike explaining things and dislike social networking, forget it.
2. If you are a technical person and don't have a clue about business and marketing, start learning. Or do a joint venture agreement with someone who has these skills.
3. If you don't like to self-promote and are constantly being modest about your skills, you will struggle, so aim to build self-promotion skills and work on your 'elevator pitch'.
4. If you think you'll just approach your ex-employer and contacts, and 'see how it goes', you're thinking too short term. Having one client is not going to work, so create a plan for reaching many more prospects.
5. If you hate learning new technology, you will not succeed as a freelancer, except perhaps as a freelance writer.

6. If you can't prioritise projects and get easily distracted during your workday, keep reading, you'll need a lot of help to make it.

7. If you hate isolation and want others to bounce ideas off of constantly, find a skilled partner, start an agency, or seek employment instead. The best-earning freelancers have had a business coach or friend in business at a higher level for support.

The Difference between Consultants and Freelancers

A **freelancer** is normally someone who is involved with the client for a specific project, which they perform off-site. They sell their services by the hour, day, or job, for a number of clients. This includes writers, graphic designers, website developers, programmers, editors, etc.

A **consultant** is given broader scope and will be guiding the client in a particular field of expertise. Often a consultant will be put on board to fix an issue. This may involve signing a contract, which may include smaller projects within it.

Continual Learning Process

> ***"The best advice I could give is … learn from those that are already successful in what you want to do. This applies to both vendors and affiliates, or anyone who is trying something they've never done before."***
>
> *- Chris Fox, eLearning, Clickbank vendor (top 1%)*

Assess Your Skills and Knowledge

But what about if you have never had any major business experience? What about if no-one has given you much of a chance? Or perhaps you've left the corporate workforce to have a baby and don't exactly know what you could do part-time from home.

Right now you need to take stock of your assets, and I'm not talking about your share portfolio! I mean your skills, contacts, portfolio, and experience. You need to plan how to use the skills and experience you have acquired, even through voluntary roles or community group participation until you get some paid clientele.

What's your story?

The story that you tell yourself might be holding you back. Is it that you need to undercut others? Is it that you need a degree and be in the 'top half' of graduates? Is it that you're too young? Not good at figures?

The most successful people I know have not had the benefit of either a full degree or super intelligence. Some of them can't even use Excel formulas to add up their finances (gasp!) – but they do know what profits they need to aim for. The story you tell yourself in your head is probably limiting your success level. But there are things you can do to change this story.

First, assess your skills from an outsider's perspective. Often it helps to have a career coach advise on how your talents can be utilised in business work. Check for Government-sponsored career advisors in your community.

Your technical skills can be put to good use as an external freelancer. Both large corporates and non-profits are increasingly less willing to hire all permanent staff. As the 'gig economy' expands, demand for skilled and talented people working remotely continues to grow. This is evidenced by a multitude of articles, e.g. *Forbes Magazine* talks about older workers doing gigs, *The Australian* talks about technical disruption and careers, and *The Herald Sun*, reporting on our digital future, asks "is freelancing the way of the future?"

If you have not got the technical skillset yet, there are many subject area courses you can take from the comfort of your home PC, e.g. on Coursera.com. The Inbound Marketing Certification course is free at Hubspot. If you decide on LinkedIn Premium (around US$49.95 per month) you'll get access to Lynda.com, where tutorials on Photoshop, InDesign, After Effects, and more, can be taken.

If you are more of a startup entrepreneur, have you ever been caught in the trap of chasing "the bright, shiny object"? That is, getting excited about the prospect of a new idea and success, but then giving up when realising the level of work required?

This is why it is so important to find your calling... and then practice the skills required like mad.

Finding Your Calling

If you like online guidance, there's free training on discovering your purpose and passion at TheEmyth.com.

Sometimes, it's hard to divine your hidden talents behind your last job's activities, or even what may interest you going forward. So look at your work history and list your skills in a general way. Find out what industries these experiences are transferable to.

If you look back on your early career and brainstorm, you may just find your special talents and what you liked to do best. When I remembered how I enjoyed writing my company's releases and web copy, I felt that freelance copywriting was perfect for me. I also turned my knowledge of self-publishing into a side business.

Setting Goals and Getting Rewarded

Before you set off, take it upon yourself to set business and personal goals that are important to you.

Ensure that your set goals are also aligned with your values, e.g. if I set a goal for making $75,000 by the end of the year from freelancing, will it be in alignment with my desire to help small businesses grow?

If your goals and values conflict, you might find yourself giving away too much time and forgetting or just not meeting your set goal.

When you really tune into what you want to do and how you want to do it and begin your action plan, then things will start going your way. The rewards will include the satisfaction of overcoming hurdles, helping others get ahead, and getting paid for something you enjoy doing.

Business Conception: Find a New Niche

Many women decide to start a business just because they want to work from home for themselves (to be close to their family) – but some don't research thoroughly enough before setting up. Sadly, some businesswomen struggle because although they know their line of work, they don't know how to promote themselves with an appropriate angle.

Even if we have passion for our work, if there isn't a defined market for it or if it's not understandable, then the business concept won't take off. So, either fill a specialised yet underserved need... or provide a new solution to an existing problem.

Use what you have already learned in your work life so far, but give it a new twist, e.g. you could specialise in training on a particular CRM with a new quick-start method.

Getting clients is the #1 problem for early stage businesses. To stand out from your competitors, create a simple, helpful process or product, something that your prospective clients will readily understand... something that helps in either solving a major problem or gaining a great benefit.

Better than a brochure, create a booklet that helps others understand the value of what you do. E.g. '5 Big Reasons to Outsource your Social Media Interactions'. Just 8-12 A5 pages or so will do, using plain language to explain it.

In this booklet, talk about how this service saves time, saves headaches, and saves money because of problems avoided. Mention your work background, to aid credibility. It's also best if you can mention a specific person or company who has been helped by you: a testimonial or an interview. Add your special intro offer at the end and contact details on the back. Give this to every interested prospect, either in person or by mail.

A great alternative to a brochure/booklet is a landing page with a simple lead capture form. This standalone page offers a tasty carrot, something that will help your niche clients in their lives. You can make this with either Landing Page software (expensive) or with the templates of a premium WordPress theme (cheaper).

Your Portfolio

Most designers, copywriters, editors, and photographers need a portfolio to showcase their work. Nowadays an online portfolio is standard and ideal to share as a link when doing a letter of offer or proposal. You can even put this link into your email signature.

Behance (https://www.behance.net/) offers a free portfolio service.

If you have a website, there are plugins (e.g. Nimble Portfolio for Wordpress) to build a beautiful portfolio without any trouble. Or some starter website builders, like SquareSpace, lend themselves to a creative portfolio. You can usually get started at a cost under $100, just to take their branding name off and get some flexibility.

Business Planning Basics

When starting such a simple business, it is tempting to fly solo without a map. But if you don't set your direction and probable cash-flow out in writing… you may be tempted back into the workforce when times get tough.

The thought of creating a business plan might give you a slight headache. Although if you are not borrowing any money, then it won't be difficult, but it will be revealing. Here's a loose guideline of what to include:

- SWOT analysis (Strengths, Weaknesses, Opportunities, Threats to your business)
- Competitor survey – include positioning and pricing
- Set-up costs, like logo design and business cards
- Ongoing costs
- Main marketing methods: how are you going to get your clients? What will that cost? Based on your pricing, what will the average client spend with you over one year?
- Likely income from services
- Likely income from products / other sources
- Future plans – what will your business be like in two to three years?

A good idea is to get a business coach or experienced business owner to have a look at your plan. They can spot any gaps or flaws in your planning. You can get some help from the BEC (Business Enterprise Centre) in your state.

In six months, come back to your plan, update it from real experience, and see what new opportunities are worth looking at.

Download a ***Business Planning template*** from Business.gov.au:

http://bit.ly/2vOdmVf

Money: Face it Now, or Lose it Later

Every business, no matter whether it is a high-cost or a low-cost consultancy, must plan these money areas:

- Income
- Profits
- Pricing
- Cash Flow and Invoicing

For many failed freelancers, too late they realised that money and cash flow were their own PRIME concern, not something to worry about at tax time.

As an employee, you thought **income** (and paying tax) was all that was important. It is still important, but *profit* is paramount, and *cash flow* is critical to your business survival. In freelancing, constant cash-flow means networking and planning for the next gigs when busy with current work.

Profit gives you a Return on Investment for any capital you put in. Profit ensures your business and you can survive – this buffer created for the hard times is called ‘operating capital’.

Pricing: You will need to bill enough to cover your costs, eventually return any starting capital, and pay yourself a decent wage. There are many hours you cannot bill for, so ensure your billable time is much higher than a full-time employee hourly wage in your geographic area.

Freelancers, your pricing should include how much time you spend in the 'selling' part of the role, plus the fact-finding and early discussions that really take time.

Cash Flow: Certain business setups will have more concerns with cash flow than others, but anyone with high overheads and debtors (clients) who are in the private sector, should pre-plan for managing cash flow.

Most 'work from home' freelance businesses require very low overheads. For the most part, your living expenses, internet, phones, brochures, and petrol will be the main costs which you know you must cover. Be clear about what you need to make to cover your costs and pay yourself a salary.

Debtors paying late or absconding? Check out the phone app: *EzyCollect*, which integrates with Xero and MYOB.

What to Do First – Tax Matters

In Australia, as in most countries, you are responsible for working out how much you can declare and claim on your tax return. You also need to be able to show how you arrived at these figures – in some cases you may be required to provide written evidence.

The first thing you need to do before getting a freelance job (if you're Australian) is apply for an Australian Business Number (ABN). If you contract for an employer *without* an ABN, they'd have to give up 40% of your earnings to the Australian Taxation Office. To apply for an ABN or GST, go to http://www.abr.gov.au/

Remember, you will need to pay income tax! So, you may figure that after the normal tax-free threshold (currently $18,000), you should put aside at least 15% of your earnings if you're not yet under a PAYG arrangement. (Please see your own country's tax tables if living outside Australia).

If you have a PAYG liability, usually you arrange to pay it in four equal instalments over the year... so knowing this, it will cause no hardship. Keep in mind your tax is assessed yearly (July to June) and your liability will probably be low the first year, especially if changing over from employee to self-employed, in that breaking-in period.

The next official year in business (after your individual tax assessment says you have earned over $2,000 from business), you should be offered the Pay As You Go (PAYG) instalments system, paying quarterly or annually towards your expected income tax liability on your business and investment income.

At the end of the tax year, any amount due to you, or tax payable, is worked out by the ATO. Your accountant can also help with pre-tax-return calculations. Aussies: look up Business PAYG instalments at www.ato.gov.au/Business

If you believe you will be earning more than $75,000 p.a. in the business, you'll need to register for GST. You can also choose to register voluntarily if you wish to (and thus you would only need to lodge once a year to start with). Check revenues each month to ensure you know your correct GST status, as you must register within 21 days of reaching the threshold.

If you are registered, to claim a GST input tax credit and claim a deduction later, you will need to keep a tax invoice for all taxable items (except for things less than $55 (inclusive of GST)). So start a file folder now for all business-related invoice PDFs.

If you're not registered for GST, you can still claim a tax deduction on the cost of goods and services (inclusive of GST), as long as they are essential to your business, for example, the cost of invoicing software. Although if you're under the tax-free threshold the first year, obviously nothing is a deduction!

Claiming Tax Deductions

Freelancers can claim tax deductions on various things that they need for work. A writer or graphic designer, for example, could claim a deduction on a new laptop. Other possible deductions might include industry magazine subscriptions, partial Internet connection costs, software, books and hardware. (Please check your own tax office for current info).

How much can you claim? This depends on the percentage of time you use the goods for work, and is subject to depreciation costs. To get it right from the start, the best thing to do is find a good accountant. Take a recommendation from a friend who is self-employed. In most cases, the savings they will find for you will more than cover their fee.

Tax Tips

- Keep your receipts. You will forget that you spent those smaller amounts, like parking or stationery and so forth, unless it's kept. For bigger purchases it's also important to keep receipts for any Tax Office audits.

- Keep good records. Use accounting software (e.g. Xero, Quicken) or an expenses app (e.g. TrackMySpend) to account for all your work-related expenditure. If you start to get a lot of work, good record keeping will become very important.

- Do you drive to clients? If your work travel is less than 5,000 km per annum, you can claim a rebate based on a cents-per-kilometre amount. If you travel more than 5,000 km you need to keep a log.

- If paper, file invoices in date order. It will be far easier to access the details if you happen to be the subject of an audit.

- Check out "Deductions Essentials" at the ATO. You may find the Home Office Expenses calculator handy, if you want to claim a portion of your home office electricity, rent or mortgage.

- If you do have an activity statement tax debt, check the current payment arrangements for the debt.

- See http://www.ato.gov.au/businesses/

What to Do First – Business Set Up

If you decide to use a name that does not contain any part of your real name, then you must register it first. See the section: *Register your Business Name*. http://www.business.gov.au/ To gain exclusive use of your name though, you have to trademark it at IP Australia.

To Incorporate or be a Sole Proprietor?

For those with a higher risk of liability and those planning to grow their business beyond themselves, perhaps with many online products, the benefits of incorporation are many. But it comes with added responsibility in the form of ASIC registration and compliance… Tax Returns which are a little more complex, necessitating more Accountant fees… and WorkCover premiums (accident compensation) for all employees (this is anyone who draws a salary).

For a quick and easy way to make a Pty Ltd company and register it, try the site: Incorporator.com.au or Google search 'Register a Company online'. However, the advice of an accountant prior to this is always a good idea!

Create invoices with an invoice template. It should include your business name, ABN or company number, contact details, GST (if applicable), an invoice number, and the name/trading name of your client.

Invoices should contain details of the work you've done (and date done) and any expenses incurred to do with the job. Save your invoices as a PDF if you send them by email.

You can also use Cloud invoicing and time tracking for multiple projects. Harvest (Harvest.com) is a subscription-based invoicing software. I use it to track the time I spend on each project and allocate time-based or project-based billing. It also works with a team.

One bonus is the reminder system for unpaid invoices, because it can automatically send email reminders for unpaid accounts every 7 or 10 days. Harvest is free for two projects or US$12.95 per month for more than two projects that are open.

Go get a separate bank account, even if you are trading under your own name. Credit Unions and building societies offer fee-free business accounts or at least low in fees. You may get a cheque book, but these days payment can be done electronically with direct transfers straight from or to your account.

Also apply for a separate Visa Debit card just for business. Why? Because many costs these days must be paid by credit card, and it's much simpler to keep records if personal and business expenses are kept separate. It doesn't necessarily have to be an official 'business account' to feature your business name, and as such need not cost anything to run. I recommend credit unions or ANZ. You'll also need a Paypal account for business.

Costs and Managing the First Year

While you may be eager to get started in business, don't skip over this, or you'll soon find costs getting away from you.

For every service there will be costs. When you set prices in your quotations, you need to cover all costs and overheads and return a profit… profit that is payment for your time. This figure should be substantially more than your past wages to account for risk, tie-up of capital (if any), and unbillable time.

There is an online program that helps you scope your projects so you don't get so many time and cost overruns. It's called Brainleaf. From $29.50 (AU $36) per month, it is ideal for website developers.

When figuring out how many weeks and hours you can bill, remember sick time, annual breaks, public holidays, and some time to cover 'breaking in' problems. Feel free to adjust to suit.

Work Out Your Billable Hours - Example:

52 weeks

- 2 weeks in public holidays

- 2 weeks in annual holidays (up to 5 weeks)

- 2 weeks in sick days or odd days off

- 10% problem days (4 weeks)

Total work weeks = 42.

Time spent:

Marketing 10-25%

Administration 5%

Professional development 5% (more if new to area)

Leaves Billable time 65-80%

Example: **Experienced Freelancer billing 30 hours per week**

$75,000 salary ÷ 42 weeks = 1785 ÷ 30 = $59.50

+ costs contingent of $288 per week (÷30) = 9.60

= $69.00 hourly rate (rounded)

Starting out, you may even be marketing your services or setting up for 90% of your time. This is why supplemental income from blog advertising or a side job can help keep you going.

The freelancer/consultant working on longer projects still needs to allocate time to running the business. Otherwise he or she will soon find themselves running short on time. So be prepared to squeeze a lot of marketing and some record keeping in between projects.

For short-term freelancers, two days per week might be spent in marketing, admin and learning, with three days for earning, in the initial stages. Of course, it is possible to run a service business part-time. But still allow 10 to 20% of that time for marketing, ongoing.

An Executive VA's Story

Cashflow is key to any business; even more so if you are a microbusiness. I didn't draw any income from my first 18 months in business. Every dollar earnt was put back into the business to pay for everything I needed to make it successful – marketing, memberships, supplies.

When I finally was able to start drawing an income from the business, it was nominal. Being a freelancer, consistency with regular projects and contracts is critical to keeping the cashflow positive. In the early days of my business, much of the work I was taking on was project-related. It took time for me to establish regular retainer clients and a steady income stream.

A low point in my second year, was a client who refused to pay. The work had been completed, she'd even commented positively about the quality of our service. With a client agreement in place, three reasonable size invoices overdue and debt collection that didn't work, I learnt a big lesson. Trust is not guaranteed in business, it must be earnt. This debt has now been written off as a learning experience!

I've now learnt to invoice promptly, follow up on outstanding invoices and at times – ask for payment in advance.

Conversations with clients about payments is never enjoyable and often put off due to the anxiety it can cause, however without income, freelancers will quickly find themselves out of business. I've learnt to overcome this by changing my mindset – I am entitled to be paid before I get started on work.

> Automating invoice reminders has also been a help in gently reminding clients of their commitment to pay for the service(s) provided. These reminders take away the awkwardness of asking for payments. These little changes have ensured my cashflow stays in the positive and I can meet my expense commitments.
>
> – *Sam Spence, Founder & Principal EA, Executive Virtual Associate*

Personal Budgeting

Most new freelancers will find themselves on a limb financially unless they plan, and include their family in this too. It may be up to you to feed the family with a mix of freelancing and other income, or it could be that your partner is going to work fulltime while you mind the kids and start your business (an even bigger challenge!).

As long as you discuss the details of what your new lifestyle will be like with your immediate family, everyone will be properly prepared.

Look at putting your yearly costs into a Budget Planner spreadsheet or app. Then, dividing that by 12, you have your monthly expenses.

Average monthly household costs in Australia range from $3,500 to $5,500 for a couple with one or two children, depending on whether you live in a city. Therefore, if reliant on this income, you would need $21,000 to $33,000 to feed yourself for the first six months. Add to that, costs of setting up the service, and we are talking about $23,000 or more at call.

Of course, you could be making money from month 2, and most freelancers do OK on a shoestring business budget.

We discuss later on various methods for creating extra income. For website or marketing people, it is beneficial to be a referral agent for software (SAAS) providers looking for new avenues to sell their products.

How much do you need? Work it out with a money app or this simple online budget planner, available from http://www.understandingmoney.gov.au.

Most freelancers under-estimate how hard it will be in the first six months to get clients who pay and keep coming back. Sometimes a few alliances with other freelancers can work out better than direct client work, as the other established design business or freelance business can send clients your way once they get to know you.

Redundancy: Plan Your Payout

- Avoid making hasty decisions about how you'll use a redundancy payment, e.g. passion projects or holidays.
- Leaving your payout in an online saver lets you earn interest at a fairly good rate, and it's still accessible.
- Be careful about using a large chunk of the payout to reduce debt. This could leave you strapped for cash if you don't attract clients and projects quickly.
- Look at your overall savings and draft up a budget to see you through around three to six months.
- If you are struggling to make interest repayments, then talk to your lender.

- Look at your skills and qualifications, and perhaps consider how you can up-skill to be relevant in the market.

Choosing a Broad Target Market

When you are thinking of contracting or freelancing to business, there are four main areas to target:

- Government
- Corporate (large business)
- Small Business
- Individuals / Entrepreneurs

Contracts with Government

To gain work for government, it is helpful to have qualifications (certification or a related degree), an understanding of how government works, a track record of working with government, and a reputation as an expert.

Generally governments publish *Request for Proposals* for specific, large projects. You will have to follow their guidelines for proposals to the letter. Then you submit your proposal and wait to hear back or wait until you are called on to present. These processes can be drawn out over a long time, or even put on hold.

In Australasia, 95% of public tenders can be seen at www.tenderlink.com. An annual subscription to the online and email tender notification service gives you access to all advertised tenders, and some exclusive tenders not published elsewhere.

A less formal way of gaining contracts is through relationship marketing. Your relationship formed with individual decision-makers in government departments will come to fruition once they have built up trust in your services and a need for your expertise arises.

Advantages:

- Always hiring, move to outsourcing
- You know they can pay
- Large contracts can sustain you financially for a long time

Disadvantages:

- Bureaucratic processes may hold up your hiring
- Large volumes of paperwork to wade through

Freelancing with Corporate Clients

Large businesses have varied requirements for hiring outsourcers – formal proposals, meetings, perhaps board approval, or maybe simply the OK of the MD/CEO.

Advantages:

- Their resources are available, and so you can charge a higher rate
- You only need a few large contracts/projects to live on
- Not as likely to have bad debts
- For marketing, the larger business is more accessible than government at a chamber of commerce meeting or industry association event.

Disadvantages of Corporate Clients:

- Perhaps some larger businesses are slow-moving and bureaucratic
- Competition is heavy!
- May be difficult to find the right decision-maker

Freelancing with Small Businesses

As this represents almost 90% of Australia's businesses, *seriously* consider this target market. There are family businesses, retail, consumer services, B2B services, and small manufacturers, so pay attention to their varied needs when you market to and service small businesses.

I have found that in the small business world, there is ample opportunity to provide advice and alternatives that will save them time and money in the long run. And because there aren't many copywriters/marketing consultants who service small clients in local areas, I focus my efforts on the small businesses around me.

Do not leave small businesses to guess at what you do. Provide lots of information and education on your area of expertise, all in plain English.

Advantages of Small Business Clients:

- Numerous small businesses can be found in your local area – not far to drive
- The market is underexploited, so your marketing attempts are not in direct competition with other outsourcers
- Less red tape to contend with, more chance of finding the appropriate decision-maker.

Disadvantages of Small Business Clients:

- Contracts/projects are smaller
- Not yet educated on an outsourcer's value and perhaps clueless when it comes to why your expertise is needed, for example, a copywriter is often met with a question about copyright or trademarks
- Must market to one business at a time
- With new businesses, more chance of a non-payer

Freelancing with Individuals / Entrepreneurs

- Simple agreement only is necessary
- Contracts will be very small
- Many soloists cannot afford your talents, so you will want to talk to the few that can
- You will have an easy affability if working for other freelancers and if starting out, they will look to you for advice.

If a novice, consider offering like-for-like barter deals with a cash-strapped solo client (for example, swap your writing of a webpage for a small advertising deal). You can still ask for a testimonial and put the project in your portfolio.

Your Positioning in the Marketplace

If you do a thorough competitor survey before entering into a service business, then you will begin to see where your positioning will feasibly lie. Here are the main variables you should consider:

- Quality of service
- Ease of process
- Pricing
- Range of services
- High or low competition at your level
- Your availability
- Your experience
- Post-service assistance

Because you are providing an intangible service, with value yet to be proven, prospective clients are looking for clues about the quality of your service. Tangibles come in the form of what the client can hear, see or experience, for example, a professional-looking website. Certain tangibles allow a level of comfort for the prospect.

Testimonials from happy clients offer good tangible proof, but there are others they need to see.

If the prospective client has taken the leap and phoned you, your availability and manner is a prime indicator of professionalism.

If your first message to them is of the "I'm sorry I cannot take the call right now, please leave a message" type, you must consider that you'll get a few hang-ups. I often wonder at the perverseness of businesspeople who give a business card with only a mobile number, but when you call that number it is switched off, and you have to leave a number by pressing #. Then the message is not responded to quickly... and the opportunity has gone.

Golden rule: ***Do not make it difficult for clients to do business with you, make it incredibly easy.***

There are many options for phone answering if you are unavailable much of the time. You can hire a 'virtual' answering service at virtual serviced offices in every city. You can choose to divert the calls (answered with your business name by a real person) to your mobile phone, or else they will send a message to you via email or SMS, for around A$55 - $85 per month.

A virtual city address for your letterhead is another option. (One I found was $75 per month). And if you have the occasional need to meet a client in the city, serviced offices have meeting rooms available for hire.

Tip: Always note your address on local business listings in Google, if it's not private. Google brings up a map for all to see, so think carefully about where it's going to be. It's a great idea to fill out your Google My Business (https://business.google.com/) profile, to gain more visibility, all for free.

Also put an address on your website, which is good for both visitors and search engines to aid with relevant search results.

Promotional Materials

Think quality! Get a decent **business card** printed with a simple design and nice colours – but don't print it yourself. If your budget is very low, online-service printers offer very cheap colour postcards and business cards. Local printers may offer $99 specials for 500 cards printed (artwork extra), on good cardstock (350gsm). Ask to see a sample first.

Putting a small picture on your card will help you be remembered, but it is optional. Explain what you do on your card, because it is your key promotional tool. You can print on the back of the card for a little extra. Perhaps your services or your positioning phrase can go there (e.g. "Coaching Your Team to Higher Performance").

Tip: Often designers of business cards can also make you an electronic business card for your email. This looks great, but just ensure that most people can still access the main details without the image.

Letterheads: First of all, will you need printed stationery? Much of our communication is via email these days. If you are printing letters, try to get it printed on 100gsm stock. If you have a really good colour printer you can do it yourself, but choose the nicest paper.

Brochures: If you are going to get a brochure printed, ensure you use a graphic designer and remember to carry across your colours, logo, and slogan/positioning statement. Speak to the reader as 'you' and do not say 'we'. There is no we, there is only you, the service provider. Try not to print too many booklets or brochures as no doubt things will change.

Media: Positioning yourself also carries across to where you promote yourself. Write an article for a glossy business magazine and you earn yourself serious credibility; tape a flyer to a lamppost and you place yourself with the Herbalife spruikers.

Your Portfolio: Keep your portfolio up-to-date with your best work. Be careful to ask the client if its OK to use their finished work in your portfolio (or put it in your terms). If you haven't done a lot of client work yet, put in colour copies of some published articles or internal pieces you've worked on (give credit if colloborative).

If you're not planning to visit prospective clients, then transfer your portfolio to your website.

Tip for Portfolio bling. If you're utilising LinkedIn, use **Behance**, a plug-in which lets you build a lovely portfolio without a website.

A good idea for either copywriters or web designers, is when you makeover a website, put a rough image of the Before website (capture the screenshot before it gets lost), together with a bigger image of the After website, along with one paragraph about why you chose to do what you did.

Fees: Your pricing also communicates your market positioning. Certain assumptions might be made from pricing alone, and you want to be sure that the client knows that they are getting value for money. Sometimes this is best left to a two-way conversation. So for this reason, many freelancers do not publish pricing.

Another reason not to publish hourly rates is that as you get faster and more experienced, you'll want some leeway to raise your prices. Hourly rates also make it tricky to charge a deposit – you'll still have to assess the length of the project if you want a decent deposit.

Always to remember to include how many revisions are included in your fee proposals.

All novice freelancers get hung up on pricing – is it too high or not high enough? In the end, if you gain trust, do a great job and add value to their business, the price won't be an objection for the right kind of client.

The odd businessperson that I've heard complaining about prices that were too high got substandard service from a provider that they did not know very well. They never even looked at their portfolio or saw any testimonials.

'Hero' Case Study:

Freelance copywriter Bob Bly is not a franchise, but he has created an empire. His 50 books, numerous eBooks, and own copywriter templates including tips on pricing, are all for sale. He repurposes his content for some of his books, and he makes use of email marketing with sales letters. His income from copywriting & consulting is over $670,000 per year.

www.bly.com

Specialties: Why are the "Riches in the Niches?"

> ***"Successful men, in all callings, never stop acquiring specialized knowledge related to their major purpose, business or profession.*** *– Napoleon Hill, Think and Grow Rich*

The marketplace rewards expertise – whether men or women. Building a specialisation is more about solving specific problems of the client than about showing how clever you are.

Robyn Haddon (Proposal strategist and writer at Flying Solo) says: "*As a soloist and a gun for hire, you're both more likely to be hired, and to be hired at a premium rate, if you are an expert in your field.*"

One of the key benefits of becoming a specialist is that repetition of familiar tasks – like writing proposals and work plans – means that you can automate your business systems, and get better and faster at what you do. You may become familiar with the automated macros in Word, for instance, and run them inside a neatly formatted template for each type of project proposed.

Some people's skills are so broad that they might think they are a generalist, e.g. HR professionals, but in fact they specialise in human resources. Conversely, project managers can apply their general skills to a varying range of areas. Once successful at managing a project on time and on budget, the project manager can go on to use that strength elsewhere.

For the virtual assistant, it is a quandary between offering a wide range of services or carving out a niche. My personal opinion is:

stress which skills area you are very good at/fast with, and you will get more of this work. Everyone knows that you can't be equally good at everything, but they still expect you to do all those common office support tasks.

So, to summarise, the first skill-set necessary to success is your **basic specialisation**.

Choosing Your Market Speciality

You may already know what kind of a specialist you will be. But there are many blends of skills that come out with a different option than you may have thought of. You may even decide that you would prefer to be a consultant, rather than a straight freelancer.

Have a good look at some of these consulting and freelancing areas:

Business Consulting (Management Consulting)

- Creating Business Plans, start-up advice
- Training and development in your expert area
- HR services: recruiting, application of regulations, payroll
- Infrastructure planning and purchasing of equipment
- Creating policies and procedures (for manuals)
- Customer relationship management and research
- Business coaching – to create better systems, client niche, and messaging overall
- Change management / Organisational development

Marketing

- Marketing planning and strategy
- Public Relations and publicity activities
- Freelance copywriting
- Freelance Graphic Design / Website Design
- SEO (Search Engine Optimisation) Consultant (may also be a copywriter)
- Internet Search Engine Marketing, PPC campaign management (i.e. Adwords, Facebook)
- SERM (Search Engine Reputation Management), Online PR and Online Reputation Management – managing an organisation brands' reputation online (usually blue chip clients)
- Social media marketing consultant (including tracking and joining dialogue about brand/company online)

Spotlight: SEO Consulting

Basically, Search Engine Optimisation (SEO) entails improving a website's listing in search engine results pages (Google, Yahoo!). In the old days (like four years ago), SEO services consisted of search phrase analysis, site analysis, copywriting and link building. These days an SEO specialist should offer a broader range of search marketing and social media services to be relevant and competitive in the ever-changing, results-driven field of SEO.

While Pay-Per-Click advertising results in short-term gains, SEO services work better over the long term.

As a consultant, you will conduct a website analysis, considering various aspects of the client's site in conjunction with Google's recommendations, you'll give clients monthly page ranking reports, and explain Google Analytics data. Start by buying good ebooks on SEO and content marketing.

Technology

- Computer programmer
- Website design and implementation (technical aspects)
- Network installation, backups, and security
- IT solutions and advice on purchase of hardware

Other

- Environmental Consulting
- Personal Efficiency & Office Organisation Consulting
- Career Counselling
- Work/Life Balance Coaching

Spotlight: Green IT Consultant

If you have a passion for the environment, then this might be one way to make a difference. Now that hardware manufacturers are promoting energy-saving 'thin client' PCs or notebooks, and most PCs can be set to power off when not in use, a consultant has ample options to advise any business on reducing their power consumption.

For general green consultants, there are a myriad of other carbon-reducing strategies that offer a win-win situation for clients.

Creative Freelancing Careers

"Follow Your Passion", experts say… Many people these days are doing just that, with their passion turned into a profitable business.

Spotlight: Specialty Freelance Writer or Blogger

Being an educated writer, you can choose to write magazine articles, white papers, ghostwriting books, witty greeting cards, or travel writing. Beware of the writer scams that want you to pay for email job lists. Find the Writer's Market guide for genuine places to sell your writing. Also make friends with busy bloggers.

See http://www.MatadorU.com for further education to become a travel writer.

If you are great at informing a target market on a subject, you will excel at ghost blogging. Many companies look for bloggers to fill the gaps in their team and create keyword-rich, interesting content. Find blogger jobs here: https://problogger.com/jobs/

Illustrator

A graduate from a design school or University, you'll have a natural flair for drawing with colour. Magazines often take on freelance illustrators for individual stories. Others find their path in book illustration, e.g. children's stories.

Colour Consultant

Working closely with the architect, you would advise on the colour choices of paint and how it works with the surrounds, including its effect on mood. Target businesses that serve the home interiors and renovations sector.

Feng Shui consultants advise on the position of furniture inside the home to garner positive moods and energy (called 'chi').

Spotlight: Freelance Photographer

Photographers often get their start with friends' weddings. You will need some good solid equipment (a Digital SLR camera, tripod, light and reflector) and knowledge of lighting.

An experienced photographer may branch into the commercial arena – for fashion, art magazines, commercial product or advertising shoots. Approach editors of magazines that seem to employ freelancers. These days even digital magazines are looking to get professional photography, especially if they're building an Instagram presence.

An outstanding photo portfolio website can also help you get a toehold in the market.

Real Estate Marketing Consultant

There are three opportunities for marketing services. A **home staging professional** is paid to de-clutter, rearrange and organize a home so that it looks its best for showing to prospective buyers.

One of the services you could supply is to create an attention-getting Open House, in which you help the Real Estate Agent ensure there are plenty of buyers showing up to see a house for sale.

A **marketing** professional would approach agents, owner-vendors and city property developers who need creative marketing materials to advertise a house or whole new development (for the latter, think luxury brochure and beautiful website).

A professional **photographer** can take the best possible pictures of furnished homes for sale, to ensure the best price. See www.Open2View.com.au for the leading Australian franchise. There are also others in this field.

Freelance Graphic Designer

Whereas you might have once designed just advertisements and corporate logos, now you can specialise in online graphics, for example, imaginative Avatars (graphical representations of people) or 3D eBook covers and subscriber form graphics.

A *multimedia designer* specialises in designing digital graphics for video games, Flash ads, or dynamic videos for business use. With the increasing use of video in many online advertising campaigns, creative and cheaper video production is a growing need.

Spotlight: Social Media Marketing Consultant

As a social media consultant, you help businesses develop and manage effective marketing strategies on social media channels, such as creating videos or managing Twitter. Sometimes a consultant would advise on search strategies or corporate blogs. Target clients would be companies who rely on Internet traffic.

The Hazards of Social Media Consulting

Be very mindful of consulting for fast-changing Internet waves like social media marketing. A social media marketing consultant admits on his blog:

> ***"You can be a gatekeeper to a new technology for a while, but you'll quickly end up being a troll trying to eek out a living guarding a bridge to nowhere, oblivious to the fact that a new bypass has opened up just down the river."*** *– Matt Granfield's blog*

Matt Granfield is a social media consultant. Besides writing a blog, he is a regular columnist for Marketing Magazine, writing on digital strategy and social media marketing. Matt has been in the digital marketing business for 13 years. He makes his living from it and yet even he realises the difficulty of trying to be a social media consultant!

However, there are forecasts that social media marketing and advertising will continue to grow. Social Media Advertising in APAC countries is expected to reach $6.7 billion by 2020, up from $2.8 billion in 2015 (Forrester Research).

Advising on Digital Marketing

As bricks and mortar businesses continue to realise the potential in marketing themselves online, many start with a "brochure" website – information that customers would normally see in the company brochure or their store. As they become more familiar with the 'digital way', they may create digital catalogues rather than print catalogues. They might set up huge blogs, with subscriber reports, or run Facebook or LinkedIn groups to encourage discussion in their business area.

Managers are now using social media to engage with consumers, such as Facebook Pages and Twitter accounts, thus expanding their customers to a wider base. Some start up an online store as part of their regular website, to tap into direct customers.

As a creative freelancer, please realise the vast potential in educating older clients from the traditional ways to promote and sell...to some of the new ways to promote and sell. For instance, how they can set up an attractive subscriber offer and email drip campaign.

This change involves willing participation or just plain curiosity from them... and ongoing learning on your part. In fact, if you don't keep learning about digital marketing and social media, you will no doubt be left behind. Most business owners now realise that they need people that know how to optimise a mobile presence or how to broaden and engage their social network audience.

The Skills of a Successful Freelancer

> ***Success is the sum of small efforts, repeated day in and day out. – Robert Collier***

The second skill set you need as a freelancer is **interpersonal skills**. Developing client relationships is imperative for successful projects. The gateway to building lasting relationships is through effective communication.

Effective communication means you listen to the clients' needs, root out some core issues while using the client's own style of language, and relate properly through words, voice tone and body language. But mainly you are listening.

If you can connect with the decision-maker on a personal level (e.g. a shared interest), this will build rapport faster than pure business talk. A key part of building rapport is giving yourself some credibility, in effect 'selling yourself'. For instance, you could relate what the person is saying (about their difficulties) back to where you have helped in a similar scenario.

Displaying self-confidence without being over-the-top or self-centred is certainly a fine art.

Other interpersonal skills you may need are: presentation skills, negotiation, and an ability to influence decisions. Influencing a room full of businesspeople is daunting for the novice. If you refine your talents in speaking to clients, and break complex things down into easy to understand metaphors or stories, then your negotiations will improve.

The third skill-set you'll need are business skills: marketing, strategy, organisation, and fair pricing. These we will address, since they are integral to any starter's success.

Reach Burnout or Start Delegating?

Sometimes we buy into the false economy that we have to do it all ourselves – be a superwoman or superman. Don't believe that you have to be expert at everything. Ask yourself, is it a better use of my time to focus on my expert area, and offload my bookkeeping or web design to someone good at this?

When you get busy you will need to start delegating. And those other service providers that you meet through networking are going to be very helpful. They are interested in helping you, and you are interested in procuring a professional service that makes your business work.

Finding Freelance Work the Easy Way

TheLoop.com.au – lists contract, permanent and some freelance jobs or gigs, mainly in Sydney and Melbourne. Help with Portfolio.

Mumbrella.com.au/jobs – Media agency based jobs - look for the orange "freelance" sign. List in the *freelance directory* as well.

Freelancer.com might offer some initial projects if you are looking for experience but they charge the project fee up-front.

TheFreelanceCollective.com.au – pay $9 per month to join high-level creatives who sometimes share project elements among them (via a closed Facebook group) or attract clients directly from the main website.

Flying Solo.com.au – while not as direct, Flying Solo offers a forum topic for "recommendations/referrals" where you can sometimes pitch your services.

Australian-only project bidding sites

www.ozlance.com.au, which is free but has fewer gigs or

www.serviceseeking.com.au (pay per lead).

While not as proliferated as the global project bidding sites, scanning local sites may reduce the time to find someone professional you can work with. I would be mindful of wasting time on Airtasker, Fiverr and those sorts of sites, because the patrons are looking for the cheapest source, not the best.

It will take a while to build up your online profile, so pick one of the large sites and give it time. (If you aim low for the first few bids, you just might get a shot).

Getting Work Fast: Advertising

The fastest and most targeted way to reach a particular market is with Pay-Per-Click advertising. This works particularly well for single products or services, but it can work for almost anything. You only pay when the searcher clicks your ad, however you need to target the *right* people.

You might know of Google Adwords™ paid advertising program. What about LinkedIn's Inmail or Premium (monthly plan)?

But first check out what you can do for free on LinkedIn. You can join up to 50 business groups and connect with members that way. Some freelancers have also grown their network through Facebook Advertising to a relevant audience, e.g. small business within 50 km. Start with giving away interesting videos or reports related to what you do.

Speaking Out

If you are learning about a specific field, such as SEO, webinars or video conferencing, then others in business will want to know too. You may find many different ways to apply your knowledge for income gain.

So build up credibility and create a little extra income with:

- Freelance writing articles for paid publications,
- Blog posts with paid advertising on the site,
- Workshops given on various niche topics,
- Speeches at local networking meetings, or
- EBook or book writing.

I recommend you join the local Toastmasters International club if you are worried about public speaking. Or read the tips at http://www.panicfreepublicspeaking.com.au/.

There are many Network Clubs and Chambers of Commerce that are looking for professional speakers. Some may pay and others may simply give valuable testimony to your services.

Don't wait for 15 years of specialised experience to make use of public speaking as a great way of gaining credibility. Start small and work your way up!

Freelance Copywriting: Insider Secrets

Like most people that start out as a freelancer, I have made a few mistakes… usually with under-quoting for multi-revision work. But I've also managed to maintain a way of life that most envy... being able to take school holidays off... write and market in 'snatches' of time.

Considering the flexibility and speed of the work, it pays well (new copywriters with workplace experience can earn $70 p/h or so). I like to charge per project for copywriting and get a 50% deposit on start. The reason to do this is that the research and communication can often take longer than the writing. *You might find the same in a lot of servicing fields.* Another reason is because having a public hourly rate is actually detrimental to you adding more value over time, as an hourly rate will be set in the client's mind.

Rather than get a mismatch of expectations of time taken and inclusions, it's better to quote it all in one figure. Never forget the time alloted for revisions and briefing.

While young bloggers might charge $10 for an article and a 20-year veteran might charge $1,000 for a home page, there's nothing to stop you from earning as much as you need, if you add value and give more great advice than competitors do.

How far you go with freelancing depends on your amount of work hours, competitors in your field, how experienced or quick learning you are, and how good you are at selling yourself. ROI also plays a role, as some copywriters can price based on proven business results.

For copywriting, qualifications are not obligatory. If you want to write for SMEs, in my opinion it's better to have worked in a small business yourself. But you'll still need to study the work of copywriting legends like Dan Kennedy, Bob Bly, Drayton Bird, Pete Godfrey... and/or attend a copywriting school. A personal copywriting mentor, like I had in my formative years, can also help.

Small business people have a practical need to control their budget, and if you provide them more 'bang for their buck', then they will come to you again. You will also be more empathetic to them.

Client Wants a 'Light Edit'

For small businesspeople, every dollar counts, and you might have to convince them that it IS worth it to rewrite the whole website rather than fiddle with edits. Because many clients are very sure their words are fine... they just need proofreading, or updating or something. This is where your outside perspective can become very useful for them… if you remind them that you are the expert in this field. Reiterate that the marketing words are the silent salesperson.

Client's Website Talks Only About Them

The most widespread problem is that the small business website copy focuses on the business longevity and its product or service features... but does not appeal to the prospect on a gut level. Stress the need to rewrite to suit the purpose and goals of the website (really you are rewriting so that the copy 'gets results').

Then find out the hidden benefits of their products/services to dot among your conversational copy, and if appropriate, add some emotional appeals.

If you are able to write in 'pyramid' style (most important points first), use commonsense phrases and direct voice, then your result will be streets ahead of most 'I did it myself' small business websites.

Specialist Positioning

You can choose to market yourself as a Marketing Consultant rather than a copywriter, adding maximum value to your client's business as you attend to their marketing materials from a broader perspective.

If you can integrate knowledge of search engine visibility, such as use of a relevant keyword phrase in copy, if you can suggest page titles, meta tags, and headings, then your website copywriting business will become SEO copywriting. SEO copywriting is highly sought after, so you can charge more for this work. It usually involves an hour more research than the average page.

The only keyword research that is free is Google Keyword Planner inside Adwords. Google has made it tricky because of secreting keywords of searchers logged into Gmail. Which is pretty much everyone.

Another way to do great research for website clients is to use a SEO overall tool. Because of the rising monthly costs of the others, and simplicity is key, when I need to build the optimisation of a website, I use Upcity.

Why are Referral Partners Better than Referrals?

The Referral Master®, Geoff Kirkwood says:

> "A referral partner is just so much better as **they do business with the same people who need your services**."

Building a referral circle involves:

- Listing the categories of businesses for alliances
- Ask them to be part of your Referral Circle
- Training each one on how to spot a good lead/referral for you.

You can get paid formal training and assistance on building alliances through *The Referral Institute* (http://www.referralinstitute.com.au), or informally by ringing around your local providers.

Marketing Your Services

> ***"An idea is an impulse of thought that impels action, by an appeal to the imagination. All master salesmen know that ideas can be sold, where merchandise cannot."*** – *Napoleon Hill*

It would be fair to say solo service providers have not got bags of spare money for advertising. Some are on a deadline of disappearing capital, while every provider needs their marketing to draw the right crowd – the paying business.

One of the best ways to market freelance services is by *networking*, either unofficially through contacts or in an official networking club. It takes time to build up contacts and instil trust, so allow at least 3 months of regular meetings before deciding if that club does work for you. Obviously offline networking is going to be more powerful than online networking, but you should try both.

You can join most online networks for free, but if you look closely they usually have a paid membership option that allows for more interaction, a featured profile, article submission, and more marketing prowess. Investigate the type of the people on the network – are they your target market?

The intricacies of your service may mean that face-to-face interaction is more effective. So choose one organisation to focus on and repeatedly put time into getting to know the regulars. As BNI members say, "Givers Gain".

Selling by Appointment

The other major face-to-face way to sell personal services is by sales appointments. To really show the person your true worth and relate on all different levels, nothing beats a personal meeting.

Firstly, ideally capture warm leads rather than cold. Warm leads would be referrals or people you've met who most likely can pay for what you supply. If you are cold calling, ensure that you qualify the prospect first; dig subtly for clues that they usually pay for services, and that prospect can afford your service.

Greet your new client with your business card, a firm handshake and a smile. Imagine them already signed up with your for a great project.

Don't assume. You are there to find out what they need and why they need it. What you must avoid in a sales meeting is trying to explain all that you know. Focus instead on what they want in the end result. Listen carefully to their language and use some of those words in your presentation.

Provide proof. After this warmer, then you need to bring to the table proof that you are good – what have people said about your services? What have you achieved for other companies? Do you have some samples to show them?

Explain briefly what you can do for them. Explain *why* it is important that you take these steps. Sell the intangibles of what they are buying for their money (i.e. better customer retention, more sales, more visible branding, more donations, etc.). Then when you come up with a project price, they are not just taking into account the COST, but the VALUE and ROI (return on investment) they receive.

Remind or ask the new client what the next step is – what do they need to do, or when will you ring them?

Case Study: A Giving Approach to Cold Calling

One tactic I used to approach small businesses was through search engine visibility. I rang up a local accountant whose site was not listed and displaying well, saying: "I noticed your site is not listing well in Google. I'm a local SEO copywriter and I may be able to help your site get found".

Because I was trying to help with a specific problem, this built trust much more than someone just trying to sell. My knowledge came across and I got the opportunity to rewrite their website text and set up their Adwords™.

Forums/Networking Platforms

www.facebook.com (Search for target client or niche topic groups)

www.linkedin.com (Business users – global)

www.flyingsolo.com.au (Australian freelancers & consultants). Haunt the forum to connect with likeminded folk who offer support and the odd referral.

Face-to-Face Networking Events:

Please see the extensive Networking list under "Learning and Growing as a Freelancer".

Find a networking event in your area by searching www.Meetup.com. Join the groups who have over 25 members and meet at least every month.

Social Media Marketing for the Freelancer

Everyone it seems is using Twitter, Facebook, LinkedIn, Instagram, and putting videos on YouTube. There are brand-minded conversations and word-of-mouth advertising going on. But is it for you?

Micro businesses, particularly freelancers, need to focus on the three best marketing tools that will bring us business, and forget the rest. *Because if you water down your efforts by trying everything at once, nothing will work.* But if you're particularly looking for research, or gaining some support for your lonely freelance journey, knock yourself out!

Social media, blogging, and linking it all up could pay dividends in page ranking and increased traffic, although not all traffic is whom you want (your target market).

Bookmarks and Tags. Delicio.us, Digg and StumbleUpon are bookmarking sites, where you will 'bookmark' your own site or blog and perhaps some affiliate sites. Tags are used in all social media to enable searchers to find certain topics, e.g. marketing. StumbleUpon traffic is not targeted enough for you as a freelancer.

Hashtags. Use hashtags, e.g. #SEO #successtips, to indicate the topic of your tweet or Facebook post. On Twitter, to send someone a message use the @theirhandle in the tweet, but on Facebook, write their name in and if linked to you, that name should appear magically; quickly hit enter to notify that person.

Social Media's purpose – the difference between social media and traditional media (press, magazines) is that social media is for sharing. It's about now – what is hot right now.

Turbo Tip: Commenting well on others' blog writing has the good effect of: a) gaining friends, and b) interesting people to go over to your blog, if a URL link of your latest post is allowed. Also try some guest posting at blogs with higher authority and high viewership (you can tell this with SEOBook tools).

Targeting Your Best Market

Really find out who your best target market could be (say local small service providers), then also choose a secondary market (say online retailers).

Part of your time you may network with similar service providers, but it is important to focus most of your efforts on your chosen target market. After all, these are the people that don't just wish they could use your talents, they NEED you urgently and they can PAY you what you deserve. So don't waste your valuable time with people just looking for free information.

Don't forget the great joint venture opportunities from working with others in an adjacent field. In a copywriter's case, website developers or graphic designers whose clients usually need copywriting services.

Turbo Tip: Promote your services with a white paper/report. A white paper is a document of three or four typed pages, which explains your position and methodology. Many companies use a white paper as a giveaway for prospects, and they have it available on their website or for subscribers. Get a professional writer to write your white paper.

Creating your own Video

Never underestimate the power of a great video for connecting across the miles. If you have no clients yet but you have expertise that you're willing to share, then plan to create a two-minute video to present yourself and your expertise to your target market.

Use this general format:

Outline a situation or problem, say what take you have on it, what action you would do, and what result would this achieve.

Make your messages as interesting and professional as you can. You will need:

- good quality video – a recent digital camera, a tripod and optionally, a lapel microphone, will be good for this;
- strong message with key benefits;

- title graphics which reinforce your message and an 'outro' (final slide with your website name) ;
- if not live, a clear voice-over.

There is now a better way to make videos from text than fiddling with editing programs. Try Lumen5 – it's so easy to upload a blog post, highlight parts you want, choose pictures, and then they compile the mp4 for you to download and share.

Now upload the video to your blog/website, YouTube, Vimeo and networking site. Choose your keywords in the title carefully – think "how to ….." or "tips for ….".

If you have no website, then send warm prospects an invitation by e-mail, with a personal message and a link to the video. Always follow this up with a phone call.

For a specific client's problems, make the video private on Youtube, or better still, put it on a USB or DVD and post it. This method is ideally suited to situations where you are targeting select high-level prospects, sometimes in another State or country. It builds trust without a lot of expense in travelling.

Another client sharing video capture tool is Jing, which allows you to send a 5 minute video from a screen capture, using their hosting. After using Jing, it automatically gives you the link to copy into an email to send. See https://www.techsmith.com/jing.html.

Your Website 101

Firstly, you might be wondering: do I really need my own website for just a service business? Yes, you do, just to compete these days. Follow my suggestions to also capture some targeted traffic. If you are going to do it, make it a professional one.

Choose a web host that provides technical support within 24 hours.

The website host will usually enable you to buy your own Domain Name from the registrar for around A$25-40 for two years. Choose a domain name which reflects your business name, ideally within your own country. Ensure you register your business name first!

Do not let a website guru you don't know take over your domain name registration! If your designer does register it, ensure they register it with your ABN and business name – we don't want legal issues later. I advise you to have all domain name and web hosting reminders sent to your fixed email address, so there are no interruptions in service (e.g. use a Gmail address for this).

Web Hosting and Design

You could pay $25 per month for hosting, if you're busy. Or you could learn how to work on website control panels, ask questions online, and only pay $7–$10 per month. Whichever you prefer.

If you are not technically minded, get a low cost website without the worry of hosting. I recommend the starter US$10 plan at Weebly.

If your needs are greater than this, e.g. you want to host videos and make it look fantastic, then host a Wordpress website.

For that I recommend Hostgator Wordpress Hosting, having used it myself. Or upgrade a little to get a SSL certificate and ensure you can collect client details or sell with privacy on-site. (Google rewards this as one of their positive ticks for your site).

Website Design – Templates

You don't have to spend $3,000 on a website design! Select from a range of stunning templates, complete with animation, customise a banner with your logo (if you're good at this) and drop in your content. I call this the wholesale way to make a website. See StudioPress, ThemeForest, WooThemes. There are great themes, like Impreza, to showcase your portfolio.

Writers are best to use WordPress (WordPress.org) to make a blog-style website with their own name or brand as the URL.

Website Planning

Targeting: Identify your target audience or users. Who are the people you would most like to visit your website?

Set Objectives: Based on the results of careful analysis, list two or three objectives for your website, e.g. "to generate leads" or "to be an updateable brochure".

Set Goals: Convert the objectives into goals that are specific, measurable, achievable, realistic and time-bound (SMART) – e.g.

"to have at least 10 visitors requesting a proposal every month by the end of my first quarter".

Plan the actions you need to take to achieve your goals. These should include drawing up or changing the specification of your website, and examining which advertising or backlinks (incoming to your site) you could create.

***Keyword research**:* If possible, ask a sample group of your target audience which words or phrases they use when searching for your kind of website or business. It is also important to know how many people actually search using each of your keywords or key phrases and how competitive these are. Use a keyword search tool for this, like Adwords' keyword planner or Upcity.

***Page structure design**:* First organise your ideas on a large piece of paper, with secondary pages feeding off menu items. This gives an overall structure and number of pages, which you can then give to your web designer for their expert input.

Assigning keywords: Assign appropriate keywords and key phrases to each web page. You will then have a different set of keywords and key phrases for each web page. A keyword can be assigned to more than one web page as long as it matches the actual content of the pages concerned.

***Web copywriting**:* Write the text for your website as if you are talking personally to a member of your target audience. Then go back and insert a few select keywords. Use hyperlinks within pages and explanatory alt tags for images. If this is too big a task for you, hire a freelance copywriter.

***Page titles**:* These play an important role in search engine positioning. Give each web page a title containing the most important keyword or key phrase assigned to that page.

***Web page design**:* Avoid Flash, as people don't want to wait for fancy graphics. Instead, focus on what your text is saying (it is your online salesperson), and ensure people return by offering clear and simple functioning. The first paragraph of each page and the first heading is important, so ensure both include your key search terms.

Also ensure your website theme is 'responsive' to mobile device use. You can test this by dragging your window across and back to see if the design adapts, then check it on your smartphone. The internal pages should end up as clear 'menu' items.

***Search engine submission*:** Don't waste your time submitting your website to hundreds of search engines and directories. Instead, submit it to local, trade association or niche market directories relevant to your business, and wait 2-3 weeks. The search engines' bots will find your website and index it to their database, but you can make it faster by submitting your site map directly (in Search Console). Also think about paying a small amount for inclusion in a major directory such as Yellow Pages®. You can also claim a free listing as well.

Beware of start-up online directories offering paid feature listings in their sites. They may be un-optimised and get little useful traffic.

***Google Analytics**:* Install this code so that you can monitor and improve your website. It allows you to review which keywords are attracting people – and see if they are staying to read (or 'bouncing' off, unimpressed). Where are the people coming from? You can check exact sources. It also has a tool to set and monitor your website objectives.

Refine your set of keywords and key phrases. Write more content on the theme of the keywords or key phrases that have attracted people (real comments, not spam).

Regular updates*:* Update the content of your website/blog at least once a month. The more frequently you update, the more often robots will visit your site, staying on your web pages to index the new material.

Testimonials from past clients build trust, so don't hide them. Put little testimonials down the side of your most frequented pages. Think of testimonials like the Referees on your CV, sometimes they represent the deciding factor in your hire.

Setting up Adwords™ to Work

You might want to start an Adwords account (with a credit voucher), but are afraid if you do it yourself you might stuff it up!

While I don't use Adwords for my own services, I find it useful for promoting books or ebooks. Here are the steps I take, but you can decide whether these are for you or not.

First, I do research on the number of keyword searches in Australia through the Google Keyword tool. When I have a shortlist of the better keyword phrases (which are usually very specific with medium traffic >10 per day), I use it to build a set of ads.

I create two ads to start, then maybe another ad group with another two ads for a different angle entirely. Some agencies make 10 ads, whatever works for the size of the project.

I integrate the highly searched for words into simple ads, each with one benefit or one problem/solution which relates to my product – a reflection of the landing page keywords.

I turn off the content network or seek specific placements, because the average click rate will be low for these ads.

I turn on manual maximum CPC, unless really short on time.

I set my daily budget at a conservative level. Remember that each click cost cannot exceed this budget.

I start out with low click prices (under the recommended bid) if I can get away with it. But I am prepared to move these up for certain targeted phrases that I think represents the best paying market.

(In some competitive fields you will not have much luck finding low click prices, e.g. web designer or accountant, but you could try typing your suburb in the keyword area, or varied specialities).

Don't forget to set your geographic area correctly. For a service business you can set it for 25 kms around your postcode – depending on how built up your area is. For products, you may set statewide or national, remembering you must have the capability to send it to where these people are.

Monitor your Adwords account weekly. Under "Reporting" you may set up an automated account or ad report to be sent to your inbox every Monday or fortnight. Also replace non-performing search terms with new ones. You will see which ones attract 0–20 impressions, and those are the ones to delete.

Blogging

As you work on becoming an expert, consider writing your own blog. It is one of the easiest ways to be published on the web – and it generates free traffic. Posts are listed in reverse chronological order, a bit like a reverse diary.

Blogs need regular updates and a central theme to focus on. Although it may take two hours a week or more of your time, there are three possible pay-offs:

1. Search engine users, some potential clients, could find your blog since it will be content-rich and niche specific.
2. It will put you in touch with other bloggers, and you will tap into what's topical.
3. Clients, colleagues, and those who learn from you will become regular readers.

Blogs are meant to reference other information – that is what differentiates them from articles. They also enable users to leave comments. (Just be sure to monitor and delete spam with a spam comment plugin).

Blogs can range from personal musings to joint efforts by journos, companies, or politicians.

While you might think of a Blog as an online diary, be extremely careful what you say, because you never know who may be reading. Even so, humour and controversy attract interest. But whether you add humour to your blog will depend on how you want to be perceived.

While journalistic articles represent a balanced perspective, blogs allow a single person to have a view about their passion. David M Scott (*The New Rules of Marketing & PR*) believes that "consumers pay attention more to these lone voices than to the pre-approved copy of company marketing." Media writers are also searching the Blogosphere for genuine stories to write up.

Simple blogging software is found on www.Typepad.com and www.WordPress.com. A blog can be set up in a few minutes, however there are some limitations to non-hosted blogs like this.

For ultimate search optimisation, you can build your website on the WordPress platform and use that to blog. Don't forget to add a few details about yourself and a small photo in the About Me section (you can also utilise a widget on the right sidebar for testimonials).

You should be able to add advertising down the side from relevant providers. Personally I didn't like the lack of control with Adsense ads, but perhaps they are getting better now. Consider adding relevant book images with links to Amazon or similar (join Amazon Associates first), so your advertising is more credible. Also partner with suppliers, like a local printer, who can pay for leads or the ad.

RSS is the format by which your regular readers can have their news delivered, so ensure that yours has an RSS feed – check the '/feed' at the end of your website URL is working OK.

> ***"All of my blogs haven't really hit their tipping point until at least a year or two into their life... so patience and creativity is important"*** *– Darren Rowse, Pro Blogger*

Turbo Tip: You can also use RSS for distribution of audio – called Podcasting. Then subscribers (having given their permission already) can receive your new seminars or radio talks onto their player automatically.

10 Reasons why Article Marketing is 'the business'

While there are many ways to boost your search engine ranking, many of them are expensive and time-consuming to get right. But if you write articles, you have a way to gain greater reach and build your credibility. Easily.

Some people seem to be everywhere at once don't they? That is because there is someone writing and repurposing their content and submitting it to article banks, Slideshare, networking sites, Twitter, as well as to their blog site.

1. **If you can write, it is free.** Traditional forms of print advertising can cost thousands of dollars to produce and place. Writing and submitting articles will only require 2-3 hours of your (or your writer's) time. Be mindful of where it is going though.
2. **Article writing shows you are an expert in your field.** People who read the articles build up trust in your name, and some may

take an interest in what you sell. They also find out more about your business speciality.

3. **Article marketing helps position your business.** Over time, your business can become well-known through customers reading articles and by clicking the URL link to your website.

4. **Articles can generate higher traffic to your website in two ways.** By writing high-quality articles and publishing on news and blog sites, you will increase links back to your website. Nowadays you need to ensure your article backlinks are from quality sites and are relevant topic-wise too, in order to improve your site's position in the search engines. You might also receive real visitors from sites, like: Medium.com, forums such as Women in Focus, and download sites like Scribd.

5. **The results are fast, and trackable.** You will be able to track incoming traffic from web publishers to see which gives you the best results (use Google Analytics or a web analytics tool). You see, the article will link back to your website, driving more traffic and potentially greater sales. Some publishers also have massive Twitter followings, so bear this in mind.

6. **Remember this yields the best results long-term.** Once your article is on the platform, it will keep bringing traffic to you website over a long duration, as editors want to keep content.

7. **They contain useful information that people on the Internet want.** If you write about solutions to common issues, whenever someone is searching for specific information that you have written about, your article will come up in a search engine.

8. **Post articles on forums and blogs to target specific customers.** Your clients share their experiences on forums or blogs, and these places can be an excellent tool for advertising softly. For instance, you can copy text to a related discussion group you have joined on Facebook.

   Comply with all rules, answer a question and then paste in the link to the full article on your blog. (Do not share from your profile as people outside your network won't see it). Some networking sites, even LinkedIn, enable you to list your articles once you have a profile page.

9. **Article writing is another search engine optimisation tool.** It allows you to use keywords and phases that are specific to your business. These keywords, placed in the body of your article and in your headings, will also get picked up by related searches in search engines or in internal searches on the article banks.

10. **Article writing helps you become a more effective educator to your customers.** While researching these articles, you will be thinking about what your customers/clients need to know, and how you can communicate the information in basic terms.

The usefulness of your content is what is going to get your article read. It must be professional and well-written, with a clear message and the right keywords.

Most people wonder if re-posting articles to LinkedIn or Medium will hurt their own website rankings. It is best to leave it two weeks before re-posting the article. Google advises:

> *"If you syndicate your content on other sites, Google will always show the version we think is most appropriate for users in each given search, which may or may not be the version you'd prefer. However, it is helpful to ensure that each site on which your content is syndicated includes a link back to your original article. You can also ask those who use your syndicated material to use the noindex meta tag to prevent search engines from indexing their version of the content."*

Don't forget to turn your article content into plain text before you submit it online. These article directories allow anyone to create a profile and submit articles:

www.ezinearticles.com

www.digg.com

Ten Commandments of Copywriting

Over half a century ago, G. Lynn Sumners, (creator of a classic magazine ad "*Imagine Harry & Me Advertising Our Pears in Fortune!*") created these 10 rules for writing winning advertisements; all of which are still applicable today:

1. **Learn all about your proposition before you write anything about it.**
2. **Organize your material from the viewpoint of the buyer's interests, not yours.**
3. **Decide to whom you are writing.**
4. **Keep it simple.**

5. **Use meaningful words and phrases – words that stir the emotions, make the mouth water, make the heart beat faster.**
6. **Don't try to be funny. Remember, the most serious of all operations is separating a man from his money.**
7. **Make your copy specific: names, places, what happens to whom.**
8. **Prove your points.**
9. **Make copy long enough to tell your story – and quit.**
10. **Give your reader something to do and make it easy for him to do it.**

Source: G. Lynn Sumners, "How I Learned the Secrets of Success in Advertising."

Topic starters:

Think of the top 5 commonly asked questions and the 5 most common problems in your field.

Write up about 500 words per topic, as if you were consulting on the problem in person.

Use the targeted keyword phrase in your #2 headings.

Add an image which explains your content. Check that it is not copyright-protected. (It could pay to have a stock photo account).

Soon you will have 10 topical niche articles ready to go.

General Creative Freelance Business Issues

The problems I have found include:

1. Work too sporadic: more proposals, communicating and marketing taking up time rather than actual billed work, leading to money troubles.

2. Thought you were getting a creative endeavour, but you find yourself mainly marketing or administrating.

3. Trying to do it all yourself means you need to be capable in skills like selling and invoicing, while focussing on being a specialist within your area.

Techniques to help with these problems:

- Create information product/s and/or workshops to supplement your income, OR

- Moonlight in a part-time job for a while, until you get established

- Outsourcing tasks to a VA or website supporter

Once you are established, the creative side will become more of your daily activity. You may decide to outsource lead generation to handle the sales if this is not your forte. Think about it carefully because you do need to use the personal touch in service businesses.

Sometimes a partner with sales skills can be the answer to low sales conversion, and it's more effective to keep sales in-house.

- For admin tasks, try outsourcing to a virtual personal assistant if funds allow, OR
- Build up your sales skills, number-crunching skills, and client liaison so that you can be self-sufficient. Learn directly from people who are really good at weaknesses of yours.

Feel the Fear in Sales, and Do it Anyway

It is very difficult to get past our modesty and fear of self-promotion, and our natural fear of rejection. Yet you need to seem confident when talking about your fees and what you can offer. And you must carry on if the prospect does not hire you, or if you get three no's in a row.

If you're not there yet, use a system of building up your positive self-talk. It can be affirmations said daily, such as "I am confident in myself and my worth".

You could also use visualisation. Think about the types of people you have served well in the past and your stand-out successes. Imagine yourself presenting the project, and them smiling and asking when you can start.

Once you focus on successes, you will be able to face a room full of people at a network group and feel confident as you say, "my strategic service adds value to my client's bottom line."

Case study: Photographer Teams Up

Julie has done a few photography projects for lone operators and online retailers, but new candidates seem loathe to pay a decent amount, thinking that their digital camera will do. She aims better and forms alliances with creative agencies. They are used to briefing for projects and hiring outsourcers, so they know the value of good creative outcomes.

With some talking about benefits and showing of her work, she agrees to a fixed fee for the agency's clientele. Julie's partnership means a new source of jobs, one that doesn't require as much persuasion.

You must realise that although some people will never value your services, when you find the *right kind* of clients, it will be a much easier task to promote yourself and your service to them.

You also need to practice an elevator pitch that can be used to tell others (anyone at all) what you do, but more importantly… what benefit you bring to them.

Using Technology in Your Service Business

A good rule of thumb to use is if the software will help you organise and keep track of your business activities, then use it. If it creates more time wastage than it saves – get a simpler system!

Programs such as Gmail/Outlook, Excel, a customer database, a simple invoicing system, and MS Word are the basic elements for my business. Adding on Adobe Creative Cloud products when needed and using a CRM has also been really handy.

An email marketing system automates all my e-mailouts and controls subscriber opt-ins. (Vision6 and MailChimp starts at free for under 2,000 subscribers).

For the business soloist, try Zoho CRM (www.zoho.com) or SugarCRM (monthly fee), as these are low-cost cloud based CRMs with features like marketing automation, mobile apps to add new contacts, notes, email handling, and more.

You might also need software for keeping track of finances and invoicing. Try the cloud-based invoicing system FreshBooks (Freshbooks.com) or the freelancer's low-cost solution, Harvest (Harvest.com) – also good for logging your hours to projects.

Creating a Supplemental Income: Money while you Sleep?

You may have read of how some internet gurus sleep while their website rakes in money for them. What you may not realise is the steep learning curve they have endured and extremely gifted copywriting skills they employ, in order to make such hefty sums. Most started off using their skills for service, but now leverage their skills into education.

So while it is not as easy as some make out, you can follow the systems set out by those successful in selling information products, tailoring it to your own niche. You can even teach others who are starting out in your field, just like this book is.

Information products can take the form of an eBook (probably the most common), how-to manual, researched report, a software program, audio (MP3), video, DVD, subscription website, webinar, or white paper. So the product can be digital or it can be made up and shipped to the customer.

Lulu.com is great for this sort of thing – it's a self-publishing site with no minimum print order, and the ability to distribute globally.

It is probably in your best interests to NOT take the easy road here and use the multinational multi-level marketing systems. Why? According to a study by the Consumer Awareness Institute, "Failure and loss rates for MLMs are not comparable with legitimate small businesses, which have been found to be profitable for 39% over the lifetime of the business; whereas less than 1% of MLM participants profit."[1]

Plus they don't add to your reputation at all. Do yourself a favour and steer clear of any system that relies on recruiting others to profit.

You need to pick an area that will build credibility for your consulting or freelancing services. You already have a passion or field of expertise, so why not help others while making an income from it?

> ***"Find your voice, don't copy someone else's"***
> ***- Seth Godin***

1 Chapter 7: MLM's Absymbly Numbers, *The Case (for and) against Multi-level Marketing*, by Jon M. Taylor, MBA, Ph.D., Consumer Awareness Institute, 2011. FTC.gov

Even if you're not a very good writer yourself, you can easily hire an editor to finesse your words, or hire a ghostwriter to completely finish your product and give you the work without taking credit. Check out Bibliocrunch (http://bibliocrunch.com).

Successful Infopreneurs

Study Those Successful at Info Marketing and Replicate

http://www.surefiremarketing.com/ Yanik Silver, US copywriter who has sold over $12 million in products!

http://www.jeffwalker.com Product Launch Formula is a system to launch any type of product. Start with his book "Launch".

One difference between digital and hard copy books, is **eBooks have more potential profit,** as the main expenses are costs that can be minimised, like PPC (pay-per-click) advertising, web-hosting and editing.

There is the choice of affiliate payment systems – which will mean having funds available to pay an online army to promote it for you. You should work in this sales or lead commission into the final ebook price. (For more information see Affiliate Store http://www.clixgalore.com.au).

With real publications, you must ensure all your printing costs are covered and there is still 50% left as a margin (or more if you want to use a distributor). You must know where you are going to sell these books and an approximate forecast of how many. Unless it is done with Print on Demand, you can easily be left holding outdated stock with no profit at all. I recommend all first-timers use Print on

Demand along with a small order for their stock.

Another difference is you won't have to wait up to two years for that book to be published… you can have it out in the market (and readily updated) in six to ten weeks!

Try Lulu.com for easy self-publishing and distribution to Apple iBooks and Nook, or IngramSpark.com (distribute everywhere, with freight in Australia) for the next level up.

Can independent eBooks sell? Look at the Amazon PageRank of eBooks on Amazon's website and you might be surprised how well many are doing. Amazon sell Kindle, but there are many other eBook reading devices, as well as smart phones and media tablets.

For print books, you can sell them direct on your website or on a standalone website with its own marketing system (e.g. a vivid 3D graphic, five hot selling points, and a bright Buy Now button, via Paypal).

Or you can utilise the retailer's sales page and offer a bookstore with those graphical links instead. See Wordpress plugin: MyBookstore.

How To and 'Dummies' style eBooks are ideally suited to the realms of business, computing and academic information, since these markets are continually changing and are high value niches.

Turbo Tip: You can sell 'How To' eBooks on iBookstore by listing them in Lulu first (ensure your price ends in .99). They do the conversion for you, as long as your sizing and formatting is standardised, or you can pay $US99+ for assisted ePub formatting.

Serious about making an income through online products?

You should begin by thinking through your objectives. Freelancing and information marketing can work well together. If you do both in harmony, it can be very profitable. Your daily work will raise problems, the solutions to which can then be turned into content and sold to a wider market.

A copywriter (or you, once trained) should write all your sales pieces, like your sales letter – a standalone web page that sells the product, website home page, pay-per-click ads, and email campaigns. The reason a copywriter can write it better, is because direct response copywriters have studied all the powerful words, the right form and order, and the headlines that sell.

Great copywriters seek to improve sales results… and that's what makes you richer!

A ***squeeze page*** is the name for a page that your target readers land on from your advert, where you convince them to opt into your e-marketing system by offering them some juicy, free information. This way you are not totally losing the large percentage of people (85%+) who are just browsing. You have a chance to let them get to know you through your emails.

Exit windows (automated pop-ups) are a great way to capture those people who were intending to leave a web page without buying. On a vibrantly-coloured screen, you tell them of your giveaway report or video series. Most of these, to work well, levy a subscription cost per year, so be wary. SumoMe Pro seems great until you pay in Australian dollars, then it is up past $300 a year.

For dual functionality, use the email marketing program **ConvertKit** (Convertkit.com), with its slide-in or modal form option and easy-to-create sequences. They have a landing page option as well, for your digital offerings. This software is around US$29 (AU$40) a month.

Lead Pages (LeadPages.net) also has a lead box pop-up in their landing page designer subscription.

Audio casts/podcasts or helpful videos can also speak to your readers more intimately, since many people learn better and retain more in an auditory or visual way. These methods have also been proven to increase responses/sales.

If you have already created a useful presentation with Apple Keynote, you can add a voiceover, adjust timing, and export it to video (mp4) to help promote your freebie or else sell the info product. I recommend Nessie USB microphones.

Your niche information product needs only a one-page website. Select a domain name carefully; perhaps something that represents your key benefit (this will also be the eBook title usually). For example, my book *Create Your New Life of Abundance* has a companion blog on www.yournewlifeofabundance.com.

One of your main objectives in information marketing should be the creation of a segmented email list. You can both educate and sell products to these warm prospects over time. Continual interaction with your list (asking questions) will help you discover people's needs, which in turn will help you choose what to sell.

The bigger your list, the more opportunities for both consulting and selling information products will come your way. You can choose to have separate lists (or tags) to keep your target markets separated. It's pretty easy. Sign-ups, de-duplication and bounces are fully automated and made legal with a good email marketing system.

People want to know you are an expert or specialist in your niche market, because they are learning from you. So:

- Mention reputable clients you have worked for, and any affiliations you may have.
- Upload a scanned copy of any newspaper or magazine article you feature in.
- Highlight any recent speaking engagements you have done.
- Use a video of yourself doing a seminar or how-to.

Turbo Tip: Offer a bonus white paper, eBook, or 7-part course for your target market, to gain their email address for further contacts (this is your 'opt-in'). Use an automated email marketing system to manage this. You will go nuts if you try to do it with Outlook, trust me! Most of the email marketing systems offer easy tutorials.

You must be visible to be a successful service professional. With all this video-making, blogging, newsletter writing, speeches, or getting published, you are building your Visibility and your Trust.

You will no longer be reliant on just referrals (although it pays to ask for these if you've completed a project well), or cold calling.

Client Loyalty and Time Management

The Nitty-Gritty Work

There is a build-up of trust gradually taking place between client and service provider, but you may be scared to ask obvious questions, such as:

- Does your client trust you?
- Is he/she able to share both positive and negative feedback about a project?
- Even if the project is meeting its original goals, does the client still view the project as valuable to his company?

These questions often get forgotten about during the course of a project, but they are important ones to find out about. The asking of feedback brings about important chances for improvement in your services or way of communicating. For instance, some people are more comfortable with the personal touch for communication, whereas others prefer emails due to restrictions on time.

And at the end of the project, if the client does seem pleased with the result, ASK for a testimonial (written or recorded on the phone). Also ask if anyone they know is having similar problems/concerns (they don't have to be asking for advice yet). This may lead to a personal referral and you can leverage off your success in this last project.

If you don't ASK, you don't get.

Providing Better Service than the Next Provider

Ric Willmot of Executive Wisdom did a survey in 2008 to find out *What's wrong in selling Professional Services in Australia.* Here is what he found, gathered from 341 clients:

- 46% of buyers state that during the process of hiring, the professional service provider failed to understand their needs.

  This, of course, highlights the wonderful opportunity for those who learn appropriate listening skills and are able to discern the needs of the buyer rather than concentrate on their own selling motives. By focusing on the client, you gain an advantage over others who do not make that same effort.

- 43% of buyers felt that the response to requests was lacking and 37% claimed the service provider was not listening properly.

> ***"To become better at marketing and selling professional services - choose something and fix it ... any improvement is an advantage!"***
> ***– Ric Willmot***

You can find out more at www.executivewisdom.com.

Ric's team is based in Carina, Queensland, Australia.

Manage Your Time... and Create More Effective Action

Time management is always critical to fulfilling our business goals; never more so than when working from home. Please take these suggestions seriously.

7 Steps to Fulfil Your Goals (by Brian Tracy)

1. First, decide exactly what you want
2. Write your goals down
3. Set a deadline on each goal
4. Make a list of every activity needed to fulfil your goal.
5. Organise this list into a Plan, by priority and sequence
6. Take action on your Plan immediately.
7. Resolve to do something every day that moves you towards your goal – e.g. call 3 prospects, read up on the subject, etc.

Don't stop! The decision to "keep going" can boost your speed of accomplishment and motivate you into motion. It can even stimulate your creativity and help you overcome procrastination.

You must decide on the best use of your time – your core genius or core strengths. Say no to everything that is not an important use of your time.

Abandon low-value tasks that are time-consuming but which provide little value to your life, so that you can focus on what's really important to you. An everyday example is reading and replying to emails (which are not urgent) intermittently. This drains your time and interrupts your thoughts. Only do that task after your project for the day is complete. Keep focussing on your most important activities.

Spending less time on unimportant activities will also free you up to spend more time with loved ones.

All these ideas are from Brian Tracy's book, *Eat That Frog*.

A Copywriter's Insight

Don't forget to take breaks from your desk – even if it's a 10-minute walk to the post box, or a cup of tea/coffee out on the patio. Your productivity will increase when you return refreshed. I've been a full-time Copywriter for 15 years now, with the last six as a freelancer. I've dipped in and out of freelance during my career but always felt pressure to conform to the 9-5, even though I HATED it!

Thing is, being a freelancer can be lonely. Everyone else you know does the 'normal' thing; has a job. Meanwhile you're sitting there on a Monday morning trying to make sense of your place in the world.

This lead to various blips of depression until finally I figured out how to make freelancing work for me.

In recent times I've been researching the psychological impacts of freelancing in terms of your professional self-image. It seemed to me that some people could just blow the competition out of the water when flying solo, while I struggled with low professional self-esteem. Again, this is all changing now and I'm adapting my business model to reflect the value I'm able to offer clients.

In short, freelancing is the best and most rewarding journey you can go on, if you're prepared for the lows and don't let them become an existential crisis.

– *Camilla Jones, Copywriting & Strategy*

Work/Life Balance for Freelancing Mothers

Whether you are looking after your little ones at home or have them looked after, a schedule is crucial to your sanity. You will find time in the early mornings or late evenings when all is peaceful, and this might be the time your creativity shines. If you can use a babysitter or Day Care for a few hours, it may work out for the best, so that you can make calls to clients and concentrate in peace.

Don't forget your need for regular exercise, healthy eating, time with friends, and even time relaxing. If you carve out time for you, it will reflect in your general demeanour and ability to focus while on the job - and also focus while with the children. A coach once advised us to have a mental closedown (eyes closed) when you close down your work computer at a set time each day.

Keeping Your Workload Full

> ***"Always build a sales pipeline that projects 3-6 months ahead – never sit back and be comfortable now you've got one job on" – G.L., Recruiter***

The failure to build new sales leads, or garner work from previous clients, will mean a gap in work – and a trough in income. A rollercoaster money flow is common in freelancing. But it doesn't have to be if you keep up your marketing activities.

A pipeline (or sales funnel) involves keeping in touch with decision-makers and noting any upcoming needs that will net you work down the track.

If you are working in a niche industry, try to protect yourself by having a cross-section of clients. Otherwise, if you have 2-3 good clients in one select area and that industry takes a downturn, you could be looking at a very dry time.

When you are incredibly busy, it is hard to take time to do face-to-face networking. But that is where you could be meeting your clients of the future, so each breakfast meeting you can get to and be present for will net results.

Being present is: taking notes, taking an interest in people there, writing their thoughts on the back of their business card, and giving them a card if they show interest. It also means following up this interest with a quick email or call a week later.

Learning and Growing as a Freelancer

Why not take advantage of the many and varied events held to educate small business people. Some are online (webinars, teleseminars), and some are offline in networking groups or workshops, where you get the benefit of networking as well.

Queensland's Small Business Solutions conduct Small Business Planning workshops (a series of 5), also with one-to-one mentoring at a heavily subsidised rate. It's really good for someone who needs a powerful start or to expand their small business. See http://www.smallbusinesssolutions.qld.gov.au (Training Events).

Also add yourself to your local Council's Economic Development and Tourism unit's business database. The business breakfasts/workshops can connect you with your local target market easily as well as having quality speakers to listen to and learn from.

Events run Nationally:

NetworxEvents.com.au – Networx Events ($75 pp)

WomensNetwork.com.au – Women's Network Australia.

www.abn.org.au – Australian Businesswomen's Network

www.businessinheels.com – Business in Heels events

Events in Brisbane Area:

https://www.meetup.com/Interactive-Minds-Brisbane/ – Interactive Minds hosts regular meetings with top marketing speakers and digital marketing mastermind events. From $75.

https://BforB.com.au – Business referral groups, meeting fortnightly, and creating referrals/alliances without pressure. Fees apply if a member.

http://www.moretonbay.qld.gov.au/events.aspx – Moreton Bay Regional Council business events.

http://www.prcc.net.au/ Pine Rivers Chamber of Commerce events and breakfast forums (Strathpine).

http://www.creativecollective.com.au – Based on the Sunshine Coast, CC offer monthly events and training days useful for learning new marketing areas.

Further Reading

Time Management:

Eat That Frog!*: 21 Great Ways to Stop Procrastinating and Get More Done in Less Time*, by Brian Tracy. 2006. Audible.

Success:

It's Not About the Money, by Bob Proctor. 2009.

The Success Principles by Jack Canfield.

You may need to buy it an audio version, because it takes awhile to absorb a 450-page book. This book refers to the *High Achiever's Focussing System*, with 7 major areas of life to achieve goals: financial & wealth, career, free time, health & appearance, relationship, personal development, community & charity.

The Wealthy Freelancer, by Slaunwhite, Savage, and Gandia, 2010. (3 free chapters at http://thewealthyfreelancer.com/)

Marketing:

The Secrets of Successful Selling, by Kristina Susac, 2004, Duncan Baird Publishers, London.

The New Rules of Marketing & PR*: How to Use News Releases, Blogs, Podcasting & Online Media to Reach Buyers Directly*, by David Meerman Scott, 2009, John Wiley & Sons.

Power Marketing: *An Aussie Guide to Business Growth*, by Jennifer Lancaster, ed.2, 2016.

Purple Cow*: Transform your Business by being Remarkable*, by Seth Godin. 2003.

The Online Copywriter's Handbook, by Robert W Bly. 2002 (Not just for copywriters, tips for all online marketers).

Optimize: How to Attract and Engage More Customers by Integrating SEO, Social Media, and Content Marketing by Lee Odden, John Wiley. 2012.

Glossary

Evergreen content

Evergreen marketing or content lasts long after its publication date because of its perennial interest. E.g. a topic such as '*Disposable nappies or Fabric nappies?*' gains interest through the years.

Curate

To curate is to collect. In content terms, this could mean bringing together a collection of content on one topic from around the web, and hosting it all in one location.

Pixel (Facebook's tracking pixel)

The Facebook tracking pixel is a JavaScript-code/image tag that you paste onto your website's pages to track website visitor's actions after they click on your ad.

Lead generation

Lead generation is about attracting and converting new customers, potentially by obtaining contact details such as email address or mobile number information. It is a tool often used to "unlock" content.

Bounce rate

A bounce rate is the percentage of single page visits where the website visitor clicked away from your site from the entrance page without browsing further. Google Analytics calculates the bounce rate of a web page from the time entered until 30 seconds pass.

> ***"A bounce rate in the range of 26 to 40 percent is excellent. 41 to 55 percent is roughly average. 56 to 70 percent is higher than average, but may not be cause for alarm depending on the website. Anything over 70 percent is disappointing for everything outside of blogs, news, events, etc."***
>
> *– The Rocket Blog at GoRocketFuel.com*

Content marketing

Content marketing is the creation and sharing of valuable content (optimised for search) in order to engage and convert prospects into customers. It could be video, an infographic, a report, or blog articles. The aim is to meet a marketing goal, whether that is brand awareness, customer acquisition or product promotion.

ROI

The return on investment metric will determine how well campaigns are performing. It varies depending on business goals (KPIs). For many, this takes the form of acquisition, such as *subscribers* or *sales leads*. Your ROI must be measurable and aligned to business goals.

RSS

Rich site summary or really simple syndication is a format for delivering syndicated web content by distributing news headlines from other sites. People are notified of new and changed content that could include news feeds, blogs, news stories and more.

CMS

A content management system is a software application that allows you to create, manage, publish, edit, archive and view content on a website. You can have authorised users publishing and managing content from anywhere at any time. Some access to the back-end is normally restricted if users are merely blog writers. A commonly used CMS is WordPress or Joomla.

Metadata

Metadata is data about data. In other words, it provides context or additional information about data explaining how and by whom data was collected and formatted. For example, it may reveal details about the methods, title, subject, author, typeface and method of compilation.

GA – Google Analytics

Not only is Google Analytics useful to look at page views, time on site and traffic trends, but it's also a great way to track where your audience is coming from. This will help you narrow down your audience and see if mobile visitors are enjoying the experience, or not. The referral source is also useful to discover where most non-Google visits are coming from. GA's *goal conversion* is a way to measure how well the website is performing, once set up and tied to an action, like the filling in of a contact form.

CTR

The Click-Through Rate is the number of clicks that your ad or content piece receives divided by the number of times it is shown. This measures the success of the ad, i.e. clicks ÷ impressions = CTR.

Say the site had 5 clicks and 1000 impressions, then the CTR would be 0.5%. While this rate tracks how much interest has been generated, it doesn't tell you the number of leads it generated. It's useful for comparing specific ad campaign responses.

Engagement rate

An engagement rate is a metric measuring the percentage of people who engaged with an ad or piece of content. Measuring your engagement rate on social media would involve looking at likes, shares, and comments (usually under 'Insights'). This allows you to better plan future social media campaigns by determining which content works and which needs changing.

UX / User Experience

User experience is about understanding how users interact with web-based systems overall – it focusess on the process and responses. If you can evaluate how a user experiences a website, for example, you can improve its usability, navigation, check-out process or calls to action.

UI / User Interface Design

UI Design is more aligned to graphic design. Being a UI specialist means you would use languages HTML and CSS to better refine the navigation, menus, layout and responsiveness of a website or app.

These two areas of UX and UI work closely together.

Resources

BEC (Business Enterprise Centre)

Find one in your area: http://becaustralia.org.au/locations/

Flying Solo www.FlyingSolo.com.au

Get support in the Forum and read useful articles.

Australian Writers Marketplace

https://www.awmonline.com.au/plans/subscription-options/

Freelance writers and authors resource. Subscribe and pay $24.95 for lifetime online access to 2,000 writing opportunities and the writing advice database.

SEO & Keyword Research Tools

If you use Firefox, download this SEO toolbar for a variety of SEO tools. http://tools.seobook.com/seo-toolbar/

Not using Firefox? Use their free keyword suggestion tools and watch the explainer video:

http://tools.seobook.com/keyword-tools/

https://adwords.google.com/KeywordPlanner – Adwords keyword search tool. Only uses predictive keyword clicks, not history.

www.goodkeywords.com – Keyword Database Manager for the Google Keyword Tool. US$49 (single user).

Social Media Types for Freelancers

Type of Network	Name	Good for
Professional	LinkedIn	Profile being found by companies, so use your keywords. If Premium account: use Inmail templates to contact decision-makers
Media Sharing	Instagram	Sharing photos, add captions, filters, mentions
Media Sharing	YouTube	How-tos, unboxing, animations, video from text
Discussion forums	Reddit, Quora, Digg	Market research, alliances
Bookmarking	Pinterest	Saving new trends, sharing images from your blogs (first optimise your feed)
Consumer review sites	wordofmouth.com.au, OneFlare	Helping new customers discover you
Blog/Publishing	Medium.com, Wordpress.com	Publish, get found, comment on ideas, share to all your profiles
Bookmarking	Twitter	Find gigs through # searches, follow/re-tweet editors' posts, find collaborators
Social Media	Facebook	Do prospect research, get a business page.

www.ingramcontent.com/pod-product-compliance
Lightning Source LLC
Chambersburg PA
CBHW061610220326
41598CB00024BC/3533

9780994510518